Published by TrailHawk Publishing, LLC
Surprise, AZ

Cover design by Ellie Starr
Interior design by Ellie Starr
ISBN: 978-1-969975-00-4

Printed in the United States of America

DISCLAIMER

This book is intended for entertainment, inspiration, and personal growth purposes only. Astrology is not a science, and the insights provided here should not be considered a substitute for professional advice. Readers are encouraged to use the information as a tool for self-reflection and empowerment, but outcomes and experiences will vary.

The author and publisher make no guarantees regarding the accuracy, applicability, or effectiveness of the practices, exercises, or interpretations in this series. Nothing in this book should be taken as medical, psychological, financial, or legal advice. For concerns in those areas, please seek guidance from a qualified professional.

By reading and engaging with this material, you accept full responsibility for your own decisions, actions, and well-being.

A NOTE FROM THE AUTHOR

The stars may offer guidance, but they don't control your destiny —
you do! Use this book as a mirror, a map, or even just a little cosmic
fun, but remember: you're always the author of your own story.

TABLE OF CONTENTS

TABLE OF CONTENTS

WELCOME TO THE ZODIAC TOOLBOX SERIES

The "Unlock Your Power: Zodiac Toolbox Series" was created to help you connect with your astrological sign in a practical, empowering way. Whether you're brand new to astrology or a lifelong star-gazer, this series is designed to be more than just information; it's a toolbox you can use for reflection, growth, and inspiration.

Inside each book, you'll find:

- An introduction to your sign: the essence of your energy and what makes you unique.
- Strengths and challenges: how to harness your natural gifts and overcome common pitfalls.
- The Toolbox: love, career, self-care, spiritual practices, and communication tips tailored to your sign.
- Planetary influences: how your ruling planet shapes your energy.
- Seasonal and monthly guidance: aligning your life with cycles of nature and the cosmos.
- Affirmations, journaling prompts, quizzes, and checklists: hands-on tools for real-life application.

Each book is meant to be interactive. Use the prompts, checklists, and reflection pages. Write in the margins. Highlight the affirmations that resonate. Make this book your own.

Remember: astrology doesn't define you; it empowers you. The stars offer guidance, but you choose the path.

PART I:
INTRO TO ASTROLOGY

WHAT IS ASTROLOGY?

Astrology is an ancient practice that looks to the heavens for meaning. For thousands of years, civilizations across the world, from Babylon to Egypt, from Greece to India, have studied the sky and noticed patterns between celestial movements and earthly events. The term "astrology" comes from the Greek words astron (star) and logos (study), literally meaning "the study of the stars."

At its core, astrology is based on the belief that there is a connection between the macrocosm (the universe) and the microcosm (human life). The positions of the Sun, Moon, and planets at any given moment reflect archetypal energies at play, and these energies often manifest in the world around us. For example, the Moon's phases are known to influence ocean tides, and many people report heightened emotions during a Full Moon.

Astrology doesn't claim to dictate our lives or erase free will. Instead, it serves as a symbolic language, a way of understanding personality traits, life challenges, and cycles of growth. Many people use astrology for self-reflection, to better understand their strengths and weaknesses, and to gain perspective during life transitions.

Astrology can be as simple as reading your daily horoscope or as complex as analyzing a detailed birth chart with dozens of planetary placements and aspects. Whether you see it as a spiritual guide, a psychological tool, or an ancient tradition, astrology offers insights that encourage deeper awareness of both yourself and the universe.

WHAT IS A HOROSCOPE?

A horoscope is like a weather forecast for your life. It is based on the positions of the planets and how their current movements (called transits) interact with your zodiac sign or birth chart. The word "horoscope" comes from the Greek hora (time) and skopos (observer), meaning "a view of the hour."

In its most common form, a horoscope refers to the Sun sign forecasts you might read online, in magazines, or in newspapers. These daily, weekly, or monthly horoscopes provide general guidance based on the characteristics of your zodiac sign. For example, an Aries horoscope might suggest taking bold action this week, while a Cancer horoscope might encourage emotional self-care.

But horoscopes go much deeper than general predictions. An astrologer can cast a personal horoscope based on the exact date, time, and location of your birth. This creates a natal chart, a snapshot of the sky the moment you entered the world. From this chart, an astrologer can interpret patterns in your personality, relationships, career, and even spiritual purpose.

Horoscopes are not about fortune-telling. Rather, they are a way to understand the energies at play in your life at a given moment. If the cosmic "weather" looks stormy, you may want to take extra care. If the skies are clear, it might be the perfect time to move forward with confidence. Just as you wouldn't cancel a trip because of rain in the forecast, you don't have to change your destiny because of a horoscope. Instead, you use it as a tool to navigate with greater awareness.

WHAT IS A ZODIAC/ZODIAC SIGN?

The zodiac is a 360-degree circle of the sky divided into twelve equal parts, each representing a zodiac sign. These signs form the foundation of Western astrology, and each one is associated with specific dates, elements, symbols, and personality traits. The word "zodiac" comes from the Greek zōidiakos kyklos, meaning "circle of animals," because many of the signs are represented by creatures such as Aries the Ram, Leo the Lion, or Pisces the Fish.

Your zodiac sign, also called your Sun sign, is determined by where the Sun was positioned on the day you were born. For example, if you were born when the Sun was moving through Aries, your zodiac sign is Aries. This sign reflects your core identity, your ego, willpower, and the way you naturally express yourself.

However, astrology goes far beyond your Sun sign. While most people know "I'm a Gemini" or "I'm a Capricorn," every individual has a full birth chart with placements in all twelve signs. Your Moon sign, for instance, represents your inner emotional world, while your Rising sign describes the way others perceive you. Together, these placements create a multidimensional picture of your personality and life path.

The twelve zodiac signs are grouped into four elements: Fire, Earth, Air, and Water. Each element represents a different style of energy. They are also divided into three modes: Cardinal, Fixed, and Mutable. These modes describe how each sign interacts with the world. By understanding the zodiac, you gain insights not only into your own sign but also into the universal cycle of growth, change, and renewal.

KEY PLANETS IN ASTROLOGY

In astrology, planets are the main characters of the cosmic play. Each planet symbolizes a different type of energy or force in life, and the way they move through the zodiac shapes our experiences. While we often think of planets as physical bodies in space, in astrology, they are archetypal energies with symbolic meanings.

- The Sun: Represents your core identity, vitality, and sense of self. It is the light you shine into the world.

- The Moon: Governs emotions, intuition, and the subconscious. It reflects your inner self and how you nurture yourself and others.

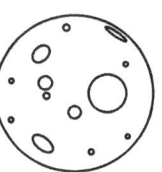

- Mercury: Rules communication, learning, and thought. It shows how you process information and express ideas.

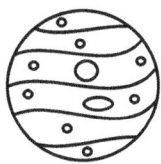

- Venus: Oversees love, beauty, money, and relationships. It describes your values, your style of affection, and what pleases you.

- Mars: Represents drive, ambition, energy, and sexuality. It is how you take action and pursue your desires.

- Jupiter: Associated with luck, wisdom, and expansion. It shows where you grow, take risks, and experience abundance.

- Saturn: Symbolizes discipline, responsibility, and life lessons. It teaches us patience and resilience.

- Uranus: Stands for innovation, change, and rebellion. It shakes things up and pushes us toward progress.

- Neptune: Rules dreams, spirituality, creativity, and illusions. It blurs the line between fantasy and reality.

- Pluto: Represents transformation, power, and rebirth. It forces us to confront what must end so something new can begin.

In astrology, Earth is not listed as a planet because it is the ground from which we observe the heavens. Instead, we look outward from Earth's perspective, and that vantage point shapes the entire astrological system.

ASTROLOGICAL HOUSES AND THEIR MEANINGS

If planets are the characters and signs are their costumes, then the houses are the stage where the story unfolds. The astrological chart is divided into twelve houses, each representing a specific area of life. The first house begins on the Ascendant, or Rising sign, and the houses proceed counterclockwise around the chart.

Here's a breakdown of the twelve houses:

1. Self & Identity – How you present yourself to the world.
2. Money & Resources – Personal finances, possessions, values.
3. Communication & Learning – Siblings, short trips, early education.
4. Home & Family – Your roots, family life, and emotional foundation.
5. Creativity & Romance – Love affairs, children, artistic expression.
6. Health & Daily Work – Routine, habits, wellness, and service.
7. Partnerships & Marriage – Romantic and business partnerships.
8. Transformation & Shared Resources – Intimacy, inheritance, shared money.
9. Philosophy, Higher Learning, Travel – Beliefs, higher education, exploration.
10. Career & Public Life – Reputation, ambitions, achievements.
11. Friendships & Community – Social groups, organizations, networks.
12. Spirituality & the Subconscious – Dreams, secrets, endings, and rebirth.

Each house acts as a container where planetary energy is expressed. For example, Mars in the 10th house may indicate someone who channels their drive into career ambitions, while Venus in the 7th house highlights love and relationships.

ASTROLOGICAL ASPECTS

Aspects are the relationships between planets, measured by the angles they form in the birth chart. These angles reveal how planetary energies interact, sometimes working in harmony, other times creating tension.

- Conjunction (0°) – Two planets close together. Their energies blend, creating intensity.
- Sextile (60°) – A supportive angle that encourages opportunities.
- Square (90°) – A challenging aspect that creates tension but drives growth.
- Trine (120°) – A harmonious flow of energy, where talents come naturally.
- Opposition (180°) – A balancing act between two forces.

Aspects are like conversations between the planets. Some are friendly and cooperative, others are tense and argumentative. A birth chart full of squares may indicate a life filled with challenges that require resilience, while a chart with many trines may feel smoother but potentially less motivating. Understanding aspects adds depth to the way we interpret astrology.

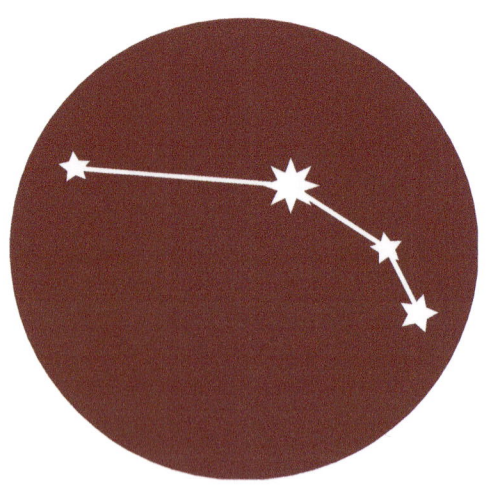

THE DIFFERENT KINDS OF ASTROLOGY

While this book focuses on Western astrology, it is just one of many traditions around the world, and these traditions can be further broken down into different branches, which have specialized applications. Each culture has developed its own system for interpreting the sky.

- Western Astrology – Uses the tropical zodiac and is most common in Europe and the Americas. It emphasizes psychological insights and personal growth.
- Vedic Astrology (Jyotish) – Originating in India, Vedic astrology uses the sidereal zodiac, which aligns more closely with the actual constellations. It places a strong focus on karma and destiny.
- Chinese Astrology – Based on a twelve-year cycle with animal signs (Rat, Ox, Tiger, etc.) and elements (Wood, Fire, Earth, Metal, Water). It is closely tied to cultural traditions and the lunar calendar.
- Mayan Astrology – Developed by the Maya civilization, this system is linked to the Tzolk'in calendar and incorporates 20 day signs and 13 galactic numbers.
- Evolutionary Astrology – A modern branch that interprets the birth chart in terms of the soul's journey, focusing on past lives and spiritual growth.

Each system provides a unique perspective, but all share a common theme: the belief that the cosmos and human life are interconnected. By studying astrology in its many forms, we see how universal the search for meaning truly is.

What first drew you to astrology? How do you feel when you read about your sign?

Do you see astrology as guidance, spirituality, or entertainment? Why?

_____

_____

_____

_____

_____

_____

_____

_____

_____

_____

_____

_____

_____

_____

_____

_____

_____

_____

_____

_____

_____

_____

_____

_____

How might learning more about your chart help you grow as a person?

_____

_____

_____

_____

_____

_____

_____

_____

_____

_____

_____

_____

_____

_____

_____

_____

_____

_____

_____

_____

_____

_____

_____

PART II:
YOUR SIGN

INTRODUCTION TO YOUR SIGN

Aries (March 21 – April 19) is the first sign of the zodiac: the trailblazer, the spark, the fire-starter. Ruled by Mars, the planet of action, Aries energy is bold, passionate, and forward-moving. You're the warrior, the pioneer, the one who dares to go where others hesitate.

MARS

You thrive on challenges, competition, and new beginnings. You're not afraid to take risks because you intuitively know that progress comes from action. Your presence inspires others to move, try, and believe.

But like fire itself, your energy needs direction and balance. Unchecked, your passion can lead to impulsive decisions, burnout, or unnecessary conflict. This book is your toolbox to help you harness your flame in a way that sustains you and those around you.

Your fire element gives you passion and spontaneity, while your cardinal modality means you're always initiating, starting fresh, and inspiring others to follow. While your drive is admirable, it's important to balance your intensity with patience and reflection.

Your Core Vibe:

"I lead. I dare. I create my own path."

ELEMENT & MODALITY REFLECTION

ELEMENT: *Fire*   MODALITY: *Cardinal*

Understanding Your Element:

As a Fire sign, Aries radiates energy, passion, and initiative. Fire fuels your drive to take action, pursue goals, and embrace life's adventures. Your enthusiasm can be contagious, inspiring others to move forward with you. However, Fire also comes with intensity: your emotions may flare up quickly, and impatience can emerge when things don't happen fast enough.

Understanding Your Modality:

Being a Cardinal sign amplifies your leadership qualities. Cardinal signs are initiators: they start projects, spark change, and pave new paths. Aries, in particular, thrives when charting your own course, breaking barriers, and taking the first step where others hesitate.

Describe a recent situation where your Aries initiative helped solve a problem or inspire someone.

_____

_____

_____

_____

_____

_____

_____

_____

_____

_____

How does your fiery energy influence the way you approach goals and challenges?

_____

_____

_____

_____

_____

_____

_____

_____

_____

_____

_____

Think of a time when impatience or impulsivity got the best of you. How could you channel that energy more constructively next time?

_____

_____

_____

_____

_____

_____

_____

_____

_____

Write three ways you can harness your Cardinal energy to create positive change in your life this month.

_____

_____

_____

_____

_____

_____

_____

_____

_____

_____

_____

_____

PERSONALITY TRAITS OF ARIES

Aries is the first sign of the zodiac, beginning the astrological cycle on the spring equinox. This makes Aries the ultimate initiator, the spark that sets everything into motion. Ruled by Mars, the planet of action and desire, Aries embodies courage, energy, and determination. They are often compared to pioneers, warriors, or trailblazers, people who refuse to wait for permission before leaping forward.

At their best, Aries are enthusiastic and inspiring leaders. Their confidence motivates others to step into their own strength. They don't just dream about ideas; they act on them. This impulsiveness can sometimes lead to mistakes, but Aries often sees mistakes as part of the learning process rather than failures.

Aries is a Fire sign, and like fire, their energy is warm, bright, and powerful. They can illuminate a room, attract followers, and energize projects. But fire must be managed carefully; when unchecked, it can burn out quickly or scorch everything in its path. Aries' impatience, quick temper, and tendency to jump from one idea to the next can cause them to struggle with follow-through.

Still, the Aries spirit is invaluable. They remind us that every great journey begins with a single step and someone brave enough to take it.

When was the last time you started something without hesitation?
How did it feel?

What role does courage play in your daily life?

_____

_____

_____

_____

_____

_____

_____

_____

_____

_____

_____

_____

_____

_____

_____

_____

_____

_____

_____

_____

_____

_____

_____

_____

In what areas could you use more patience to balance your fiery energy?

_____

_____

_____

_____

_____

_____

_____

_____

_____

_____

_____

_____

_____

_____

_____

_____

_____

_____

_____

_____

_____

_____

_____

UNLOCKING YOUR STRENGTHS

Aries, your greatest power lies in your courage, enthusiasm, and drive. You excel in situations that require leadership, decisive action, or pioneering new ideas.

Key Strengths & How to Use Them:
1.) Courage: Take risks and face challenges head-on. You move forward even when others hesitate. Use this to pursue bold career moves or personal growth opportunities.
→ USE IT: Tackle new opportunities, ask for what you deserve, speak up.

2.) Passion: When you commit to something, your energy is contagious. You bring enthusiasm into everything you touch. Channel it into creative projects or relationships.
→ USE IT: Inspire your friends, coworkers, or community to rise to your level.

3.) Leadership: Others naturally look to you for guidance. People look to you because you're unafraid to take the first step. Harness this to inspire teams, mentor friends, or create communities.
→ USE IT: Lead by example, but practice listening as much as acting.

Exercise:
List three areas of your life where fear is holding you back. Write down the first bold action you can take in each and commit to completing it this week.

<u>Area 1:</u>

<u>Area 2:</u>

<u>Area 3:</u>

OVERCOMING CHALLENGES

Even strong Aries energy can face pitfalls: impatience, impulsivity, and occasional stubbornness. Your greatest challenges mirror your greatest strengths. Your fire burns bright, but sometimes too fast. Recognizing these tendencies is key to growth.

Common Challenges:
- Impulsivity and acting before thinking, which can cause unnecessary conflicts
- Struggling with patience when results aren't immediate
- Overcommitting due to enthusiasm
- Stubbornness can lead to difficulty backing down

Strategy:
Practice "pause and plan" exercises: Before making a big decision or reacting in anger, take three slow breaths, write down the pros and cons, and then act. Combine with your natural boldness for balanced results. This tiny pause helps you transform raw fire into focused power.

When was the last time you acted impulsively? What was the outcome?

_____

_____

_____

_____

_____

_____

_____

_____

_____

_____

_____

_____

_____

_____

_____

_____

_____

_____

_____

_____

_____

_____

_____

_____

Which situations trigger frustration or impatience in you?

_____

_____

_____

_____

_____

_____

_____

_____

_____

_____

_____

_____

_____

_____

_____

_____

_____

_____

_____

_____

_____

_____

_____

_____

How can you pause before reacting next time?

_____

_____

_____

_____

_____

_____

_____

_____

_____

_____

_____

_____

_____

_____

_____

_____

_____

_____

_____

_____

_____

_____

_____

_____

How can you reframe patience as power instead of weakness?

_____

_____

_____

_____

_____

_____

_____

_____

_____

_____

_____

_____

_____

_____

_____

_____

_____

_____

_____

_____

_____

_____

_____

_____

What beliefs do you cling to that no longer serve you?

THE ARIES TOOLBOX

<u>Love & Relationships:</u>
- Best matches: Leo (shared fire), Sagittarius (adventure), Libra (balance)
- Communication tip: Be honest, but temper intensity with empathy. Remember, passion is great, but patience keeps the fire alive.
- Self-check: Are you giving your partner space while maintaining connection?
- Challenge: Avoid dominating or rushing partners.

<u>Career & Money:</u>
- Ideal careers: Entrepreneur, athlete, innovator, project leader
- Money tip: Invest in your passions but avoid impulsive spending or job-hopping, and pair your big ideas with long-term planning.
- Work style: Take initiative, set bold goals, and celebrate achievements.

<u>Self-Care Rituals:</u>
- Physical activity: High-energy workouts or outdoor adventures.
- Creative outlets: Start a new hobby or creative project each month.
- Relaxation: Meditate, spend quiet time in nature to recharge, stretch, or journal.

Aries

RELATIONSHIP & COMPATIBILITY

COMPATIBILITY OVERVIEW:

MOST HARMONIOUS:

Leo, Sagittarius, Gemini, Aquarius

POTENTIALLY CHALLENGING:

Cancer, Capricorn, Libra

Love & Romance:

Aries loves boldly and passionately. You are adventurous in love, often drawn to partners who can keep up with your energy and enthusiasm. Independence is crucial, both for yourself and your partner. You thrive in relationships where excitement, spontaneity, and mutual respect for personal freedom exist.

Friendships & Social Life:

You are loyal, direct, and protective of your friends. Aries friends are the ones who will show up for you without hesitation and encourage you to step out of your comfort zone. At times, your blunt honesty may unintentionally hurt others, so reflection and empathy are key.

Family:

In family dynamics, you may take on a leadership or protective role. You love nurturing others through action rather than words, but your fiery temper can create conflicts if not managed carefully.

Think about a relationship (romantic, friendship, family) where your Aries passion shone. How did it positively impact the connection?

_____

_____

_____

_____

_____

_____

_____

_____

_____

How do you balance your desire for independence with the needs of others?

_____

_____

_____

_____

_____

_____

_____

_____

_____

_____

_____

Write a short note (for your eyes only) to someone you care about, expressing your appreciation or intention to strengthen the bond.

_____

_____

_____

_____

_____

_____

_____

_____

_____

Identify one trait in a partner or friend that sparks your excitement and one that challenges you. How can you navigate both gracefully?

_____

_____

_____

_____

_____

_____

_____

_____

_____

_____

_____

_____

CAREER & MONEY

IDEAL CAREERS:

Entrepreneurs, athletes, military leaders, surgeons, firefighters, creative directors

Why These Fit:

Aries' confidence and quick decision-making are assets in high-stakes environments. They enjoy competition, taking risks, and seeing immediate results.

Money Mindset:

Aries often spend as fast as they earn. They're impulsive shoppers but also highly resourceful when motivated. They thrive with short-term financial goals rather than long-term ones.

How can you balance your adventurous spirit with financial discipline?

_____

_____

_____

_____

_____

_____

_____

_____

_____

_____

_____

_____

What risks are you willing to take to achieve financial independence?

_____

_____

_____

_____

_____

_____

_____

_____

_____

_____

How can you balance your adventurous spirit with financial discipline?

_____

_____

_____

_____

_____

_____

_____

_____

_____

_____

_____

_____

SELF-CARE RITUAL

Aries tend to burn themselves out because of their high energy. A self-care ritual for Aries should focus on balancing fire with calm, channeling excess energy, and recharging.

The Aries Fire Reset Ritual:

1. Movement Release – Do 15 minutes of fast-paced activity (dancing, boxing, jogging) to burn off adrenaline.
2. Cooling Shower – Take a lukewarm shower, visualizing red-hot energy washing down the drain.
3. Essential Oils – Apply peppermint or eucalyptus oil to the temples and wrists to calm fiery energy.
4. Candle Meditation – Light a red candle. Sit in stillness for 5 minutes, focusing on the flame. Breathe deeply, imagining the flame transferring its energy into your core.
5. Affirmation – Repeat: "I channel my fire into purpose, not exhaustion."

What activities drain your energy the fastest?

_____

_____

_____

_____

_____

_____

_____

_____

_____

_____

_____

_____

How can you recharge without feeling guilty?

_____

_____

_____

_____

_____

_____

_____

_____

_____

_____

When was the last time you truly rested without distraction?

_____

_____

_____

_____

_____

_____

_____

_____

_____

_____

_____

_____

ARIES

Spiritual Growth:
- Rituals: On the New Moon, set bold intentions. On the Full Moon, release impatience.
- Strengths: Courage to begin, passion, energy, authenticity, leadership in spiritual spaces.
- Growth: Develop patience, balance ego with humility, learn to rest, turn impulsiveness into mindfulness.
- Affirmations: "I am bold. I am capable. I lead my own journey."

Communication Hacks:
- Practice active listening before responding.
- Use direct but compassionate language.
- Reflect before reacting to heated situations.
- Use "I feel" instead of "You always."
- Channel passion into constructive feedback.

THE SYMBOL OF ARIES

The symbol of Aries is the Ram, an animal known for charging forward with determination. The Ram is one of the most ancient and enduring symbols in astrology, and it is no coincidence that it was chosen to represent Aries, the first sign of the zodiac. The ram's horns curve outward, representing both physical strength and the spiritual ability to break through barriers. In ancient times, the ram was associated with fertility, renewal, and sacrifice, which ties into Aries' role as the sign of new beginnings.

The Ram captures the spirit of Aries perfectly: bold, determined, and fearless in the face of challenges. The ram also reflects the Aries personality: strong-willed, brave, and unafraid of confrontation. When a ram wants something, it pushes relentlessly until it achieves its goal. Similarly, Aries often approaches life headfirst, sometimes without considering obstacles, but always with a bold spirit. But the Ram is not just an image of brute force; it carries centuries of mythological, cultural, and symbolic weight that illuminates the essence of this fire sign.

THE MYTHOLOGICAL ROOTS OF THE RAM

In Greek mythology, the Ram is most famously tied to the story of the Golden Fleece. According to legend, the golden ram named Chrysomallos was sent by the gods to rescue two children, Phrixus and Helle, from danger. The ram carried them through the skies, demonstrating courage, speed, and the willingness to sacrifice for others. Later, when the ram's fleece was hung in a sacred grove, it became the coveted prize in the epic tale of Jason and the Argonauts. This tale symbolizes courage, leadership, and the pursuit of greatness, which are all core Aries traits.

For Aries, this myth conveys several key themes: bravery in the face of adversity, leadership that inspires others, and the pursuit of seemingly impossible goals. The ram's heroic act of flight and sacrifice parallels Aries' natural drive to forge ahead, protect loved ones, and tackle challenges others might shy away from.

THE RAM AS A SYMBOL OF STRENGTH AND DETERMINATION

Rams are known in the natural world for their physical strength and persistence. With their curved horns and headstrong nature, they climb rocky mountainsides and battle rivals for dominance. This raw determination reflects the Aries spirit: a refusal to give up, even when the climb is steep. Aries natives are often trailblazers, embodying this resilience in their careers, relationships, and personal pursuits.

The ram's horns also symbolize power and protection. Just as a ram uses its horns to defend itself and claim its place, Aries individuals often use their fiery personalities and confidence to carve out a path in the world. There's a readiness to stand up, to fight for beliefs, and to take risks where others might hesitate.

CULTURAL AND SPIRITUAL INTERPRETATIONS OF THE RAM

Beyond Greek mythology, the ram has appeared as a sacred animal in cultures around the world. In ancient Egypt, the ram was associated with Amun-Ra, the god of creation and fertility, symbolizing vitality and the life force. In Celtic traditions, the ram represented renewal, rebirth, and the turning of seasons, an echo of Aries' placement at the start of the zodiac, marking new beginnings with the arrival of spring.

This broader cultural symbolism highlights the ram not only as a creature of strength but also as a spiritual force tied to growth, transformation, and the courage to step into the unknown. Aries energy, too, embodies these qualities, urging individuals to embrace change and initiate new ventures without hesitation.

WHY THE RAM REPRESENTS ARIES

Aries is the first sign of the zodiac, ruled by the fiery planet Mars, which governs action, drive, and conflict. The ram embodies this same forward-charging energy. Just as a ram lowers its head and rushes toward a goal with unwavering intensity, Aries individuals approach life with bold enthusiasm and determination.

The ram's symbolism also reminds Aries natives of their natural leadership abilities. They are often the ones to go first, to clear a path, and to inspire others to follow. This pioneering quality makes them natural innovators, risk-takers, and visionaries; always ready to climb the next mountain or chase the next horizon.

In what areas of your life do you feel most like a ram: determined, strong, and unstoppable?

_____

_____

_____

_____

_____

_____

_____

_____

_____

_____

_____

_____

_____

_____

_____

_____

_____

_____

_____

_____

_____

_____

Where in your life are you ready to charge forward, even if obstacles stand in your way?

_____

_____

_____

_____

_____

_____

_____

_____

_____

_____

_____

_____

_____

_____

_____

_____

_____

_____

_____

_____

_____

_____

_____

_____

The ram is also tied to sacrifice and protection. Who or what would you fiercely protect, and why?

_____

_____

_____

_____

_____

_____

_____

_____

_____

_____

_____

_____

_____

_____

_____

_____

_____

_____

_____

_____

_____

_____

_____

PLANETARY POWER INFLUENCES

Aries is ruled by Mars, the planet of drive, ambition, and raw energy. This gives you courage, initiative, and stamina, but it can also make you restless.

- Mars in Daily Life: You need movement. Without projects, workouts, or goals, your energy can turn into frustration.
- Mars in Relationships: You're passionate but sometimes competitive. Channel that energy into adventure together rather than arguments.
- Other Planetary Influences can amplify your natural tendencies or highlight areas for growth:
    - Moon: Reminds you to slow down and nurture yourself emotionally.

    - Venus: Softens your edges and deepens intimacy.
    - Mercury: Shapes your fiery communication, but beware of Mercury retrograde frustrations.

    - Saturn: Teaches patience and discipline; the yin to your Mars yang.

Reflection: How can you align your drive (Mars), voice (Mercury), and vision (Sun) so they all move in the same direction this season?

_____

_____

_____

_____

_____

_____

_____

_____

_____

_____

_____

_____

_____

_____

_____

_____

_____

_____

_____

_____

_____

_____

_____

_____

DAY(S) OF THE WEEK FOR ARIES

Each zodiac sign resonates strongly with certain days of the week, and for Aries, that day is Tuesday, named after Tiw (or Tyr), the Norse god of war, and linked to Mars, the Roman god of battle and passion. This isn't by chance. It's rooted in ancient traditions that connected days with planetary rulers. Tuesday is ruled by Mars, the same fiery planet that governs Aries itself. This alignment makes Tuesday the perfect expression of Aries energy: bold, decisive, and brimming with action. Tuesday is considered the most action-oriented day of the week, a perfect match for Aries energy. This makes Tuesdays ideal for Aries to tackle their biggest challenges, start new projects, or take bold steps forward. The fiery energy of Tuesday complements Aries' natural drive, giving them extra momentum to move through obstacles.

THE LINK BETWEEN MARS AND TUESDAY

The connection between Tuesday and Mars goes back to the Romans. In Latin, Tuesday was known as dies Martis, or "the day of Mars." In other languages, this connection is even clearer:

- In French, Tuesday is mardi (literally "Mars' day").
- In Spanish, it's martes.
- In Italian, martedi.

Mars, the god of war in Roman mythology, represented courage, battle, and unyielding strength, which are all qualities that Aries embodies. When Mars' day comes around each week, Aries natives feel a natural boost in confidence, vitality, and motivation to tackle challenges head-on.

WHAT TUESDAY MEANS FOR ARIES

For Aries individuals, Tuesday is more than just another day on the calendar; it's a natural reset button for ambition and determination. While others might dread the early part of the week, Aries thrives on the fiery push that Tuesday provides. It's a day for new projects, bold decisions, and breaking through obstacles.

Aries often experiences Tuesday as the perfect day for:
- Taking initiative – starting that new project, pitching a big idea, or making a tough phone call.
- Physical activity – workouts, sports, or anything that gets the blood pumping, align perfectly with the Mars energy.
- Leadership – Tuesday encourages Aries to step up, take charge, and guide others with confidence.

HARNESSING THE ENERGY OF TUESDAY

Because Tuesday amplifies Aries traits, it can be a powerful day for rituals, planning, or even self-reflection. Aries can harness this energy by:
- Scheduling important meetings or launches on Tuesdays.
- Using the day for self-discipline, turning raw enthusiasm into focused action.
- Practicing grounding activities like journaling or meditation after high-energy bursts to prevent burnout.

For Aries, Tuesday is a reminder that they are natural initiators. The universe gives them a weekly "power day" to align with their ruling planet and make things happen.

BALANCING THE FIERY ENERGY

Of course, with great power comes great responsibility. Tuesday's Mars-driven force can sometimes push Aries toward impatience, aggression, or impulsiveness. It's important for Aries natives to be mindful of this and balance their day with calming practices, such as deep breathing, creative outlets, or connecting with nature. By learning to channel Tuesday's fiery spark in constructive ways, Aries can maximize productivity without letting tempers flare.

How do you usually feel on Tuesdays compared to other days of the week? Energized, drained, or neutral?

_____

_____

_____

_____

_____

_____

_____

_____

_____

_____

_____

_____

_____

_____

_____

_____

_____

_____

_____

_____

_____

_____

What important task or decision could you schedule on Tuesdays to harness Mars' influence?

When has your natural Aries drive on a Tuesday helped you succeed or move forward?

_____

_____

_____

_____

_____

_____

_____

_____

_____

_____

_____

_____

_____

_____

_____

_____

_____

_____

_____

_____

_____

_____

_____

_____

How might you balance the fiery energy of Tuesday with grounding practices?

LUCKY NUMBERS FOR ARIES

Every zodiac sign resonates with certain numbers that amplify its energy, and for Aries, those numbers reflect leadership, action, and bold beginnings. These lucky numbers serve as cosmic signatures that align with Aries' fiery personality and ruling planet, Mars. While luck is never guaranteed, Aries often finds that these numbers appear at key moments in life, offering guidance, confidence, or a gentle nudge toward success.

THE PRIMARY LUCKY NUMBERS FOR ARIES

The numbers most often associated with Aries are 1, 9, and sometimes 6. Each of these numbers carries a vibration that speaks to the Aries spirit in different ways.

- Number 1 - The Pioneer: Number 1 is the number of beginnings, originality, and leadership. It reflects Aries' role as the first sign of the zodiac: bold, innovative, and unafraid to chart a new course. Aries often thrives when they embrace the "number one" energy: being first, standing out, and trusting their instinct to lead rather than follow.
- Number 9 - The Warrior: Number 9 is closely tied to Mars, Aries' ruling planet. In numerology, 9 represents drive, ambition, and completion of cycles. For Aries, this number energizes their fighting spirit, pushing them to achieve their goals and to defend their passions. It also carries a humanitarian streak, reminding Aries that true strength is not only about winning battles but also about uplifting others.
- Number 6 - The Harmonizer: Though less obvious, number 6 is sometimes linked to Aries for balance. While Aries tends to rush headlong into life, the number 6 brings themes of responsibility, care, and harmony. This influence helps Aries soften their fiery nature and use their leadership skills to nurture and protect rather than dominate.

HOW LUCKY NUMBERS WORK FOR ARIES

For Aries, lucky numbers are not just mystical trivia. They can serve as daily reminders of strengths, potential, and alignment with cosmic forces. Some Aries individuals may notice these numbers repeating in addresses, phone numbers, dates, or significant milestones. When they appear, it often feels like a subtle confirmation that Aries is on the right path.

Practical ways Aries can harness their lucky numbers include:
- Choosing important dates (for launches, weddings, or travel) that feature these numbers.
- Incorporating the numbers into rituals, like repeating affirmations 9 times or lighting 1 candle to represent a fresh start.
- Using them as motivational markers. For example, setting a 9-day challenge to push toward a personal goal.

THE ENERGY OF NUMBERS IN DAILY LIFE

Aries thrives when their environment supports their natural energy. By intentionally weaving their lucky numbers into daily routines, they create an atmosphere of focus and empowerment. A house number, locker combination, or even a lucky charm with one of these numbers can serve as a small yet powerful reminder of Aries' resilience and fiery drive.

A WORD OF BALANCE

While lucky numbers can offer Aries encouragement, it's important not to rely solely on them. They are meant to amplify natural strengths, not replace effort, discipline, or preparation. True luck for Aries comes when their fiery determination meets the right opportunities, and the numbers simply highlight moments when the universe aligns in their favor.

Which numbers seem to reappear in your life? Do they hold meaning for you?

_____

_____

_____

_____

_____

_____

_____

_____

_____

_____

_____

_____

_____

_____

_____

_____

_____

_____

_____

_____

_____

_____

Think about a time when one of your lucky numbers appeared at a turning point. Did it influence your decision or outcome?

_____

_____

_____

_____

_____

_____

_____

_____

_____

_____

_____

_____

_____

_____

_____

_____

_____

_____

_____

_____

_____

_____

_____

_____

_____

_____

How can you intentionally weave your lucky numbers into your daily routines or personal rituals?

_____

_____

_____

_____

_____

_____

_____

_____

_____

_____

_____

_____

_____

_____

_____

_____

_____

_____

_____

_____

_____

_____

_____

_____

Do you feel most aligned with the leadership of 1, the strength of 9, or the harmony of 6? Why?

_____

_____

_____

_____

_____

_____

_____

_____

_____

_____

_____

_____

_____

_____

_____

_____

_____

_____

_____

_____

_____

_____

_____

_____

FLOWERS OF ARIES

Every zodiac sign has flowers that resonate with its unique energy, and for Aries, those blooms reflect passion, vitality, and renewal. Aries, as the first sign of the zodiac and a fire sign ruled by Mars, bursts with life force and bold energy. The flowers connected to Aries embody this fiery spirit, reminding us of courage, beginnings, and the will to thrive even in challenging conditions.

THE PRIMARY FLOWERS FOR ARIES

The flowers most closely associated with Aries are the honeysuckle and the thistle. Both bloom early in the season, marking the arrival of spring, the natural domain of Aries. They symbolize not only new beginnings but also resilience and strength.

- Honeysuckle – Sweet Vitality: Honeysuckle blooms in early spring, climbing and twining its way toward the sun. This plant mirrors Aries' ambitious and upward-reaching nature. Its sweet fragrance speaks to Aries' ability to draw others in with charm and magnetism, while its persistence reflects Aries' determination to rise above obstacles. Honeysuckle is also a flower of love and protection, highlighting Aries' loyalty to those they care about deeply.
- Thistle – Fierce Beauty: The thistle, with its spiky exterior and vibrant purple bloom, represents both the toughness and the beauty of Aries. Just like Aries, the thistle is not afraid to stand tall and protect itself while still offering something striking and vibrant to the world. It symbolizes bravery, resilience, and the readiness to defend what matters most. The thistle's message to Aries is clear: strength and sensitivity can coexist.

THE SECONDARY FLOWERS FOR ARIES

Other flowers often linked to Aries include geraniums, tiger lilies, and red tulips. These blooms carry fiery colors, reds, oranges, and bold pinks, that reflect Aries' dynamic and passionate personality.

Each flower reinforces a different aspect of Aries energy:
- Geraniums – Represent protection and confidence.
- Tiger Lilies – Stand for boldness and pride, echoing Aries' flair for individuality.
- Red Tulips – Symbolize declarations of love and passion, aligning with Aries' open-hearted nature.

THE DEEPER SYMBOLISM

Aries' flowers are not only visually striking but also deeply symbolic of this sign's role in the zodiac. Aries marks the beginning of the astrological year, and its flowers remind us of rebirth, fresh starts, and the courage to bloom brightly in a world that is still shaking off winter's slumber.

These flowers also reinforce Aries' connection to the element of fire. Their vibrant colors and ability to thrive with energy and vitality parallel Aries' own fiery spark. To surround oneself with these flowers is to invite courage, initiative, and motivation into daily life.

HOW ARIES CAN USE THEIR FLOWERS

Aries individuals can benefit from consciously incorporating their flowers into rituals, décor, or self-care practices:
- Fresh Bouquets: Place honeysuckle, thistle, or tulips in your workspace to inspire motivation and new ideas.
- Bath Rituals: Add petals from Aries flowers to a warm bath as a cleansing and energizing ritual.
- Affirmation Pairing: While meditating or journaling, keep an Aries flower nearby as a visual reminder of your resilience and passion.
- Gift-Giving: When choosing flowers for an Aries loved one, opt for these bold, fiery blooms; they'll feel instantly seen and understood.

Which Aries flower resonates most with your personality:
honeysuckle's charm, thistle's resilience, or tulip's passion?

_____

_____

_____

_____

_____

_____

_____

_____

_____

_____

_____

_____

_____

_____

_____

_____

_____

_____

_____

_____

_____

_____

_____

How do you express your own version of "fierce beauty," balancing strength with vulnerability?

_____

_____

_____

_____

_____

_____

_____

_____

_____

_____

_____

_____

_____

_____

_____

_____

_____

_____

_____

_____

_____

_____

_____

_____

_____

Imagine your life as a garden in bloom. What qualities or achievements would each Aries flower symbolize for you?

How might you use flowers in a personal ritual to encourage fresh beginnings or courage?

_____

_____

_____

_____

_____

_____

_____

_____

_____

_____

_____

_____

_____

_____

_____

_____

_____

_____

_____

_____

_____

_____

_____

_____

FAMOUS ARIES INDIVIDUALS

Studying well-known Aries can provide real-life examples of Aries traits in action.

- Lady Gaga (March 28) – Fiercely creative, unapologetic, and fearless in breaking boundaries, she embodies Aries' trailblazing spirit.
- Robert Downey Jr. (April 4) – Charismatic, witty, and resilient, his career comeback reflects Aries' ability to bounce back stronger than ever.
- Maya Angelou (April 4) – Her bold voice and powerful words show Aries' courage in speaking truth.
- Mariah Carey (March 27) – Known for her powerhouse voice and confident presence, she reflects Aries' flair for drama and passion.

These individuals highlight Aries' leadership, creativity, and unwillingness to be silenced.

Which famous Aries inspires you the most, and why?

_____

_____

_____

_____

_____

_____

_____

_____

_____

_____

_____

_____

ARIES MAN VS. WOMAN

Aries energy expresses itself differently depending on gender identity, cultural expectations, and individual personality. While both Aries men and women are ruled by Mars and embody the fiery, pioneering spirit of the Ram, their approaches to love, ambition, and relationships often take on unique flavors.

THE ARIES MAN

The Aries man is bold, enthusiastic, direct, adventurous, and confident. He tends to approach life like a battlefield where victories are won through courage and determination. With a restless energy, he is rarely content with standing still. He thrives on competition and challenges, and loves the thrill of the chase. He is drawn to experiences that test his strength. In relationships, he is passionate and direct; if he likes someone, he doesn't hide it. However, his impulsive nature can make him impatient, and he may struggle with long-term planning.

In Love & Dating: The Aries man is passionate and impulsive. He loves the chase, often pursuing partners with intensity. He appreciates spontaneity in romance and is quick to express interest. However, his fiery passion can sometimes fade as quickly as it ignites, which means he needs a partner who can keep him engaged intellectually and emotionally. Aries men value honesty and excitement. They want partners who can keep up with their energy and independence. Expect surprises, adventure, and spontaneous gestures.

In Sexuality: He is fiery, adventurous, and confident in intimacy, often bringing enthusiasm and energy into the bedroom. For him, passion and physical connection are inseparable from emotional involvement. Aries men enjoy passion without too much complication.

Trustworthiness: The Aries man values honesty but can sometimes be impulsive in ways that test relationships. When committed, though, his loyalty is fierce, though his impulsiveness may make him seem unpredictable. He thrives with partners who encourage his independence without making him feel restricted.

Understanding Him: To truly understand an Aries man, one must recognize his need for both freedom and validation. He seeks admiration for his courage and initiative, and he responds best to partners who can keep pace with his adventurous spirit.

Gift Ideas: The Aries man enjoys gifts that fuel his passions: sports gear, adventure experiences, bold fashion accessories, or anything that makes him feel like a trailblazer. Gadgets, adventure gear, bold fragrances, or experiences like tickets to a concert or sporting event.

ARIES MAN VS. WOMAN

THE ARIES WOMAN ♀

The Aries woman is equally fiery but expresses her energy with a unique blend of independence, confidence, charisma, drive, and charm. She is often seen as a natural leader, unwilling to compromise her freedom for a relationship that doesn't honor her strength. She is a trailblazer in her own right, often unafraid to challenge norms and carve her own path. Dynamic and inspiring, she embodies the pioneering nature of Aries with fierce determination.

In Love & Dating: The Aries woman is magnetic and bold, often taking the lead in romance. She values independence and respects partners who admire her strength without trying to control her. She is drawn to excitement and thrives in relationships that offer passion and adventure. She wants a partner who respects her autonomy and ambition. She values directness; playing games is a quick way to lose her interest. Expect high energy, fun, and spontaneity.

In Sexuality: She approaches intimacy with confidence and directness. Passionate and energetic, she seeks a partner who matches her enthusiasm. She is adventurous and unafraid to express her desires. Emotional authenticity is important. She quickly loses interest if intimacy feels routine or insincere.

Trustworthiness: The Aries woman values honesty and transparency. She expects straightforward communication and has little patience for games. Though her fiery temper may flare, she forgives quickly when trust is genuine. Once she chooses someone, her loyalty is fierce. But she demands the same in return.

Understanding Her: The Aries woman thrives when she feels

respected for her independence. She needs space to pursue her passions and becomes frustrated if she feels stifled. She appreciates partners who celebrate her boldness and see her as an equal.

Gift Ideas: The Aries woman enjoys gifts that highlight her individuality and energy: bold statement jewelry, unique fashion pieces, fitness gear, bold clothing, adventure trips, or experiences that let her showcase her fiery spirit.

SHARED TRAITS & KEY DIFFERENCES

Both the Aries man and woman are pioneers at heart, fueled by Mars' fiery influence. They share courage, determination, and a zest for life. However, their differences lie in expression:

- The Aries man often channels his energy outward through action, competition, and pursuit.
- The Aries woman blends action with self-expression, often challenging norms and leading by example.

COMPATIBILITY CONSIDERATIONS

- Aries Man in Relationships: Needs a partner who can balance his impulsive nature with grounding energy, while still fueling his adventurous side.
- Aries Woman in Relationships: Needs a partner who respects her independence, admires her strength, and joins her in creating excitement.

How do you express your Aries energy differently from others of your sign?

_____

_____

_____

_____

_____

_____

_____

_____

_____

_____

_____

_____

_____

_____

_____

_____

_____

_____

_____

_____

_____

_____

_____

What qualities do you value most in love, and how do they reflect your Aries nature?

_____

_____

_____

_____

_____

_____

_____

_____

_____

_____

_____

_____

_____

_____

_____

_____

_____

_____

_____

_____

_____

_____

_____

What kind of gifts or experiences make you feel most alive?

_____

_____

_____

_____

_____

_____

_____

_____

_____

_____

_____

_____

_____

_____

_____

_____

_____

_____

_____

_____

_____

_____

_____

_____

Think about a time you felt misunderstood in love. Was it because of your fiery Aries nature? How did you explain or handle it?

_____

_____

_____

_____

_____

_____

_____

_____

_____

_____

_____

_____

_____

_____

_____

_____

_____

_____

_____

_____

_____

_____

_____

THE ARIES MONTHLY & SEASONAL GUIDE

Aries is the first sign of the zodiac, ruled by fire and Mars, so your energy rises and falls with the seasons. Think of each season as a new phase for your fire: sometimes blazing, sometimes glowing softly, sometimes needing rest.

Spring: ARIES IN FULL BLOOM (MARCH – MAY)

This is your season; the New Year of the zodiac. You feel unstoppable and motivated with high energy, and ready to start fresh. This time is ideal for starting new projects. Bold moves and risk-taking come naturally.

- Focus Areas: Fresh starts, leadership, courage, vision
- Power Moves: Launch projects, set bold goals, step into leadership roles
- Challenge: Burning out by doing too much, too fast

"Spring awakens my courage. I honor new beginnings."

What fresh start are you most excited to take this spring?

_____

_____

_____

_____

_____

_____

_____

Where can you channel your courage to create something new?

_____

_____

_____

_____

_____

_____

_____

How can you prevent burnout while chasing new goals?

_____

_____

_____

_____

_____

_____

_____

SPRING FOCUS AREAS:

SPRING POWER MOVES:

SPRING CHALLENGES:

"Summer fuels my fire with joy and connection."

Summer: ARIES IN ACTION (JUNE - AUGUST)

Summer amplifies your fiery energy. Adventure, fun, and spontaneity call to you. Relationships heat up, and you thrive in movement, travel, and play.

- **Focus Areas:** Connection, adventure, passion, creativity
- **Power Moves:** Try new experiences, deepen relationships, travel or explore
- **Challenge:** Impulsivity, overspending, or scattered focus

Fall: ARIES IN REFLECTION (SEPTEMBER - NOVEMBER)

Autumn invites you to slow down and recalibrate. It's a season of harvest, reaping what you've sown since spring. Reflection and planning become essential.

- **Focus Areas:** Balance, evaluation, grounding, preparation
- **Power Moves:** Review progress, adjust long-term goals, practice patience
- **Challenge:** Resisting the slowdown, feeling restless when things calm down

"Fall grounds me. I reflect, release, and prepare for what's next."

How can you embrace adventure while staying grounded?

_____

_____

_____

_____

_____

_____

_____

What relationships deserve more of your energy this summer?

_____

_____

_____

_____

_____

_____

Where do you want to explore new opportunities?

_____

_____

_____

_____

_____

_____

_____

SUMMER FOCUS AREAS:

SUMMER POWER MOVES:

SUMMER CHALLENGES:

What successes are you most proud of from this year so far?

_____

_____

_____

_____

_____

_____

_____

_____

Where can you adjust your plans for better results?

_____

_____

_____

_____

_____

_____

_____

_____

What habits or patterns are you ready to release?

_____

_____

_____

_____

_____

_____

_____

_____

FALL FOCUS AREAS:

_____

_____

_____

_____

_____

_____

_____

_____

_____

_____

_____

_____

_____

_____

_____

_____

_____

_____

_____

_____

_____

_____

_____

_____

_____

_____

_____

_____

FALL POWER MOVES:

FALL CHALLENGES:

_____

_____

_____

_____

_____

_____

_____

_____

_____

_____

_____

_____

_____

_____

_____

_____

_____

_____

_____

_____

_____

_____

_____

_____

_____

_____

_____

_____

_____

_____

Winter: ARIES IN RENEWAL (DECEMBER - FEBRUARY)

Winter calls you inward. It's a time for rest, self-care, and spiritual growth. Your fire softens into embers that keep you warm but remind you to pause and restore.

- **Focus Areas:** Healing, renewal, inner strength, rest
- **Power Moves:** Reflect, recharge, and dream big for the year ahead
- **Challenge:** Feeling restless or guilty for slowing down

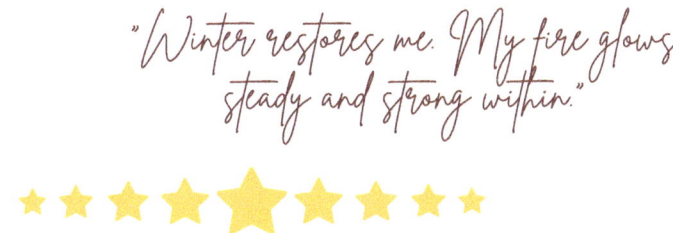

"Winter restores me. My fire glows steady and strong within."

⭐ ⭐ ⭐ ⭐ ⭐ ⭐ ⭐ ⭐ ⭐

Mini-Roadmap:
Each month, pick one area of focus: career, self-care, relationships, spiritual growth. Align it with your energy level and planetary influences.

How can you give yourself permission to rest this winter?

_____

_____

_____

_____

_____

_____

_____

What does renewal look like for you?

_____

_____

_____

_____

_____

_____

_____

What seeds of intention are you planting for the year to come?

_____

_____

_____

_____

_____

_____

_____

_____

WINTER FOCUS AREAS:

WINTER POWER MOVES:

WINTER CHALLENGES:

ACTION PLAN: ARIES POWER WEEK

7-Day Challenge:

- Day 1: Identify one bold goal and why you want to achieve it.
- Day 2: Break it into small, actionable steps.
- Day 3: Declare your intention aloud.
- Day 4: Take the first step.
- Day 5: Reflect on progress, adjust as needed.
- Day 6: Celebrate small wins.
- Day 7: Journal about lessons learned and next steps.

Power Playlist/Resources:
- Music: "Don't Stop Me Now" (Queen), "Eye of the Tiger" (Survivor), "Can't Hold Us" (Macklemore & Ryan Lewis)
- Books: "The 5 Second Rule" by Mel Robbins, "You Are a Badass" by Jen Sincero
- Crystals: Carnelian, Red Jasper, Clear Quartz
- Colors: Bold reds and fiery oranges

Day 1 Reflections

Identify one bold goal and why you want to achieve it.

_____

_____

_____

_____

_____

_____

_____

_____

_____

_____

_____

_____

_____

_____

_____

_____

_____

_____

_____

_____

_____

_____

_____

_____

Day 2 Reflections

Break it into small, actionable steps.

_____

_____

_____

_____

_____

_____

_____

_____

_____

_____

_____

_____

_____

_____

_____

_____

_____

_____

_____

_____

_____

_____

_____

_____

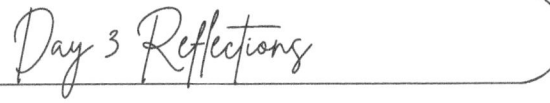

Day 3 Reflections

Declare your intention aloud.

_____

_____

_____

_____

_____

_____

_____

_____

_____

_____

_____

_____

_____

_____

_____

_____

_____

_____

_____

_____

_____

_____

_____

_____

_____

_____

Day 4 Reflections

Take the first step.

_____

_____

_____

_____

_____

_____

_____

_____

_____

_____

_____

_____

_____

_____

_____

_____

_____

_____

_____

_____

_____

_____

_____

_____

_____

Day 5 Reflections

Reflect on progress, adjust as needed.

_____

_____

_____

_____

_____

_____

_____

_____

_____

_____

_____

_____

_____

_____

_____

_____

_____

_____

_____

_____

_____

_____

_____

_____

_____

Celebrate small wins.

_____

_____

_____

_____

_____

_____

_____

_____

_____

_____

_____

_____

_____

_____

_____

_____

_____

_____

_____

_____

_____

_____

_____

_____

_____

Day 7 Reflections

Journal about lessons learned and next steps.

_____

_____

_____

_____

_____

_____

_____

_____

_____

_____

_____

_____

_____

_____

_____

_____

_____

_____

_____

_____

_____

_____

_____

_____

_____

_____

_____

AFFIRMATIONS & MANTRAS FOR ARIES

Love & Relationships:

- I give and receive love with passion and patience.
- I honor my partner's voice as much as my own.
- My fiery heart brings warmth and joy to my relationships.
- I let love flow without rushing it.
- I am worthy of deep, lasting connections.
- My independence strengthens, not threatens, my love life.
- I practice patience as an act of love.
- I attract partners who celebrate my courage and spirit.
- I release the need to control and embrace harmony.
- Love is a flame that grows brighter with trust and respect.

Write about a time when listening deeply strengthened a relationship.

_____

_____

_____

_____

_____

_____

_____

_____

_____

_____

_____

_____

_____

_____

_____

_____

_____

_____

_____

_____

_____

_____

_____

_____

_____

_____

How do you bring warmth and joy into your connections?

_____

_____

_____

_____

_____

_____

_____

_____

_____

_____

_____

_____

_____

_____

_____

_____

_____

_____

_____

_____

_____

_____

_____

_____

_____

_____

How does your independence benefit your relationships?

AFFIRMATIONS & MANTRAS FOR ARIES

Career & Money:

- I am bold in pursuing my career dreams.
- Every risk I take is an opportunity to learn and grow.
- I turn my passion into purpose and prosperity.
- I balance ambition with patience for long-term success.
- I am capable of leading with wisdom and strength.
- Money flows easily when I act with intention.
- I trust myself to make smart financial choices.
- My ideas spark opportunities that others value.
- I follow through on my goals with focus and fire.
- Abundance comes when I align my work with my purpose.

Self-Care:

- I honor my body by moving it with strength and joy.
- Rest fuels my fire, and I allow myself to pause.
- I release stress through healthy outlets that energize me.
- My vitality grows when I balance action with stillness.
- I deserve care, compassion, and nurturing.
- My energy is sacred, and I spend it wisely.
- I honor my limits without guilt.
- Self-care is not selfish; it is strength.
- I protect my peace as fiercely as I protect my goals.
- My body and mind work together to sustain my fire.

What bold career move are you ready to take?

Write about a time when a risk led to growth.

What does true leadership mean to you?

How do you feel when you move your body with strength and joy?

_____

_____

_____

_____

_____

_____

_____

_____

_____

_____

_____

_____

_____

_____

_____

_____

_____

_____

_____

_____

_____

_____

_____

Write about a time that you showed yourself compassion.

How does caring for yourself help you care for others?

_____

_____

_____

_____

_____

_____

_____

_____

_____

_____

_____

_____

_____

_____

_____

_____

_____

_____

_____

_____

_____

_____

_____

_____

_____

_____

_____

CHECKLIST 1: ARIES SELF-CARE HABITS

Use this checklist weekly to balance your intensity:

☐ I moved my body in a way that energized me.

☐ I practiced patience at least once today.

☐ I took 5-10 minutes to pause and breathe before reacting.

☐ I drank enough water to fuel my fire.

☐ I journaled about my emotions instead of bottling them up.

☐ I connected with someone who supports me.

☐ I celebrated a small win this week.

☐ I said "no" when I needed to protect my energy.

☐ I scheduled downtime to rest and recharge.

☐ I ended my day with gratitude.

☐ I moved my body in a way that energized me.

AFFIRMATIONS & MANTRAS FOR ARIES

Spiritual Growth:

- I trust the universe to guide my bold steps.
- My inner fire connects me to divine energy.
- I am open to wisdom from both action and stillness.
- The cosmos fuels my courage and resilience.
- I grow spiritually every time I act with intention.
- My intuition is strong and trustworthy.
- I embrace the lessons hidden in challenges.
- The universe rewards my bravery with new paths.
- My spirit is an eternal flame: powerful, purposeful, divine.
- I align my actions with my higher self.

Communication:

- I speak with clarity and kindness.
- My words inspire and uplift others.
- I listen deeply before responding.
- Passion in my voice is a strength when guided with care.
- I release the need to win arguments and choose connection.
- My honesty creates trust in my relationships.
- I channel my fire into empowering conversations.
- I express myself with confidence and compassion.
- I use my voice to encourage, not to harm.
- My communication builds bridges instead of walls.

Write about a time when stillness brought unexpected wisdom.

_____

_____

_____

_____

_____

_____

_____

_____

_____

_____

_____

_____

_____

_____

_____

_____

_____

_____

_____

_____

_____

_____

_____

_____

_____

_____

_____

_____

_____

What lessons have challenges taught you about growth? *Spiritual Growth*

_____

_____

_____

_____

_____

_____

_____

_____

_____

_____

_____

_____

_____

_____

_____

_____

_____

_____

_____

_____

_____

_____

_____

_____

_____

What spiritual practices keep you grounded and inspired?

CHECKLIST 2: ARIES POWER MOVES

Keep this as a monthly guide to stay aligned with your sign's strengths:

- [ ] Start something new (project, hobby, or idea).

- [ ] Take one courageous risk.

- [ ] Practice patience with a long-term goal.

- [ ] Set clear boundaries around my energy.

- [ ] Use my voice to inspire or encourage someone.

- [ ] Spend time outdoors to recharge.

- [ ] Track my progress and celebrate milestones.

- [ ] Align my goals with my higher purpose.

- [ ] Honor rest as fuel for my next big move.

- [ ] Reflect on where my fire is helping and where it's overwhelming.

Where can you choose connection over "winning" an argument?

Write about a time when listening changed your perspective.

What bridges do you want to build with your communication?

_____

_____

_____

_____

_____

_____

_____

_____

_____

_____

_____

_____

_____

_____

_____

_____

_____

_____

_____

_____

_____

_____

_____

_____

_____

_____

_____

_____

_____

QUIZ 1: AM I IN MY ARIES POWER OR ARIES SHADOW?

Answer Yes / Sometimes / No to each statement:

1. I take bold action on my ideas without hesitation.
2. I often act before I've thought things through.
3. People see me as inspiring and motivating.
4. I get impatient when results don't come quickly.
5. I stand up for myself and others with courage.
6. I struggle to slow down or rest.
7. I bring passion and energy to my relationships.
8. I sometimes speak before I think, and it causes conflict.
9. I see challenges as opportunities to grow.
10. I find it hard to let go of control.

Results:

Mostly Yes to odd numbers (1, 3, 5, 7, 9): You're living in your Aries power — courageous, inspiring, and full of drive. Keep balancing your fire with patience.

Mostly Yes to even numbers (2, 4, 6, 8, 10): You're leaning into your Aries shadow — impulsive, restless, or reactive. Focus on grounding practices to regain balance.

Mixed: You're in transition. Reflect on where fire helps you and where it burns too hot.

QUIZ 2: WHAT KIND OF ARIES ARE YOU?

Choose the option that best describes you:

1.) When facing a challenge, I:
- a) Jump in headfirst
- b) Take a breath, then act
- c) Step back and wait

2.) My favorite way to spend energy is:
- a) Competing or leading
- b) Exploring new adventures
- c) Helping others grow

3.) My biggest strength is:
- a) Courage
- b) Passion
- c) Creativity

4.) My biggest challenge is:
- a) Impulsivity
- b) Impatience
- c) Stubbornness

5.) My ideal motto is:
- a) "Fortune favors the bold."
- b) "Slow and steady wins the race."
- c) "Together, we rise."

Results:

Mostly A's: The Warrior – Bold, fearless, unstoppable. You light the path.

Mostly B's: The Explorer – Adventurous, curious, open-minded. You inspire discovery.

Mostly C's: The Visionary – Creative, determined, focused. You make ideas a reality.

PART III:
ACTIVITY PAGES

Doodle Your Constellation: Draw the Aries constellation as you imagine it in the night sky. Include stars, lines, or imaginative elements like flames, mountains, or arrows; symbols of your fiery, pioneering spirit.

YOUR IDEAL ADVENTURE

Manifestation Map: Create a visual map of your dream journey: physical, emotional, or spiritual. Include places you want to explore, goals you want to conquer, and experiences that ignite your fire. Use words, drawings, or symbols to make it vivid.

<u>Fire Energy Release Exercise:</u> Draw or write about something that has frustrated or blocked your energy recently. Then, create a symbolic act of release (e.g., drawing flames, scribbling boldly, or listing ways to let go). Reflect on the sensation afterward.

<u>Creative Writing Prompt:</u> Imagine you are the hero of your own story. You have just received a call to adventure that will test your courage, leadership, and spontaneity. Write the first scene in your journal. What is your challenge, and how do you rise to meet it?

_____

_____

_____

_____

_____

_____

_____

_____

_____

_____

_____

_____

_____

_____

_____

_____

_____

_____

_____

_____

_____

_____

_____

_____

Mapping Your Cosmic Blueprint:

Your Sun sign (like Gemini, Aries, Taurus, etc.) is only one piece of who you are. Your birth chart, sometimes called a natal chart, is a snapshot of the sky at the exact moment you were born. It shows where all the planets were, revealing your deeper layers of personality, emotions, desires, and life lessons.

What You'll Need:
- Your birth date, birth time, and birth city.
- Access to a free online chart generator (such as Astro.com, CafeAstrology.com, or Astro-Seek.com).

Steps to Create Your Chart:
1. Visit one of the free astrology websites listed above.
2. Enter your full birth details and select "Natal Chart" or "Birth Chart."
3. When your chart appears, take a screenshot or write down where each planet is located (for example: Moon in Libra, Venus in Taurus, Mars in Leo).
4. On your paper, draw a circle to represent the chart. Divide it into 12 sections. These are the houses.
5. Label each house starting with House 1 (Ascendant) and move counterclockwise.
6. Add symbols or keywords for each planet in its corresponding sign and house.
   - Example: ☉ Sun in Gemini (House 10: Career)
   - ☽ Moon in Cancer (House 11: Friendships)

YOUR BIRTH CHART

What patterns do you notice in your chart? (Are many planets in Air signs? Water signs?)

_____

_____

_____

_____

_____

_____

_____

Which signs or elements dominate your chart, and how do they influence your energy?

_____

_____

_____

_____

_____

_____

_____

Where is your Moon and Rising sign? How do they balance or amplify your Sun sign?

_____

_____

_____

_____

_____

_____

_____

PART IV: WRAP-UP

CONCLUSION

Aries, you are the pioneer of the zodiac; the spark that lights the fire for new beginnings. Your courage, drive, and passion give you the power to create a life filled with bold achievements and personal victories. But your true mastery lies not only in your ability to charge forward, but in learning when to pause, reflect, and allow your inner fire to burn steadily rather than consume everything in its path.

Think of your journey as a balance between fire and fuel: your energy is limitless when managed wisely. By using this book's tools, embracing your strengths, reflecting on your challenges, and practicing self-care rituals, you are building a sustainable flame that will light the way not only for yourself, but for everyone inspired by your leadership.

Aries, you are a natural leader, a pioneer, and a fearless adventurer. Your toolbox equips you to harness your innate power, navigate challenges, and thrive in every aspect of life. Remember: the stars guide, but you lead.

Aries, you are both spark and flame. The world looks to you for inspiration, courage, and energy. But your true gift is balance: knowing when to ignite, when to rest, and when to guide others with your light.

By working with this toolbox, you transform your natural boldness into a life of purpose, joy, and resilience. Keep leading with heart! The stars may guide you, but the fire within you lights the way.

"I am a bold pioneer. I act with courage and wisdom. My fire is eternal, and I choose how it burns."

RESOURCES

Astrology & Self-Discovery:
- "The Only Astrology Book You'll Ever Need" by Joanna Martine Woolfolk
- "Astrology for the Soul" by Jan Spiller
- "The Twelve Houses" by Howard Sasportas

Journaling & Mindfulness:
- "The Artist's Way" by Julia Cameron
- Insight Timer (free meditation app)
- Daylio or Journey (journaling apps)

Crystals & Energy Tools:
- Carnelian (courage + confidence)
- Red Jasper (grounding + stamina)
- Clear Quartz (clarity + focus)

Online Resources:
- www.astro.com – free birth charts and reports
- www.cafeastrology.com – astrology basics and guides
- www.chani.com – astrology app and resources
- www.horoscope.com
- www.zodiacsign.com

NOTES:

NOTES:

NOTES:

NOTES:

NOTES:

NOTES:

ABOUT THE AUTHOR

Ellie Starr is a writer, intuitive guide, and lifelong student of the cosmos. With a passion for blending ancient wisdom and modern self-development, she created the "Unlock Your Power: Zodiac Toolbox Series" to help readers harness their natural strengths, overcome challenges, and live with purpose.

When she's not writing, Ellie can be found stargazing, journaling with a cup of tea, or exploring new ways to connect with the rhythms of the universe. She believes that astrology is not about fate, but about empowerment; a mirror that helps us see ourselves more clearly.

Through her work, Ellie invites you to embrace the spark of your fire nature, to lead with courage, and to burn brightly with passion and purpose. Just as fire lights the way, you too can ignite inspiration and transformation in your life.

Stay connected with Ellie Starr:
Website: www.trailhawkpublishing.com/elliestarr

www.ingramcontent.com/pod-product-compliance
Lightning Source LLC
Chambersburg PA
CBHW051315120626
46547CB00015B/2252